KIDD
ROCKS

ROLLING WITH
JASON KIDD
AND THE
NEW JERSEY NETS

Mark Stewart
and
Mike Kennedy

TRIUMPH
BOOKS
CHICAGO

All photos courtesy
AP/World Wide Photos, Inc.
except the following:

Brian Spurlock — Page 6
Steve Lipofsky — Pages 28, 30, 33, 41
Jake Lemle — Pages 38, 39

The following images are from the
collection of Team Stewart:

College Sports Publishing © 1992 — Page 8
Classic Games © 1994 — Page 8 inset
Sports Illustrated/TIME INC © 1993 — Page 9
The Upper Deck Company © 1994 — Page 12
Sports Illustrated for Kids/TIME INC © 2000 — Page 13
Beckett Publications © 1995 — Page 14
PRIMEDIA Specialty Group © 2002 — Page 18
Dr. Pepper © 1974 — Page 31
Daily News © 2002 — Page 41 inset

CONTENTS

1 SOME KIDD

They say that beauty is in the eye of the beholder. Anyone who saw Jason Kidd run the point for the New Jersey Nets in 2001–02 would have a hard time disagreeing. The 29-year-old point guard, bestowed upon the formerly hapless franchise by the Phoenix Suns, took the long-anticipated final step in his basketball career and elevated his game to a championship level. And as Jason ascended, so too did the Nets. It was a beautiful thing to watch.

After fashioning the best record in the East, the Nets gained experience and confidence in victories over the Indiana Pacers and Charlotte Hornets in the playoffs. In the conference finals, Jason played the Celtic defense like a Stradivarius, and stepped up time and again when Net fans feared the team was about to quit. At this unlikely place, on this unlikely team, in this unlikely uniform, Jason Kidd

> "I thought he was the greatest guard to come out of high school since Magic Johnson."
>
> • **Lute Olson, Arizona coach**

Jason roots on his teammates during a Nets win. The team spirit and leadership he brought to New Jersey had been years in the making. Jason was considered a basketball "prodigy" during his teen career in California.

Jason locks in on an enemy point guard during a college game.

grasped that which had eluded him for nearly a decade: unquestioning respect...and a shot at basketball's brass ring.

The road from the Oakland 'burbs to the NBA Finals had once seemed preordained for California's most famous child hoops prodigy. There were articles penned about Jason's prowess while he was still in grade school. He had the thing you can't teach, people said; he knew what his teammates were going to do and where they were going to be, often before they knew themselves. And he was totally unselfish.

> " Jason Kidd is the only player I've seen in 32 years of coaching who could possibly skip college and go straight to the NBA. "
>
> **• Jim Harrick, UCLA coach**

That rarest of combinations earned Jason a unique status on the asphalt of Oakland's parks and playgrounds. He was from Alameda, the "right" side of the tracks, which meant he was an automatic outsider. Seriously, the Kidds owned horses. But the playas recognized Jason's genius, knew he could make them better, and brought him into their world. There he encountered a bruising mentor named Gary

Payton—class of the Class of '86 at Skyline High and star of the Oregon Ducks.

Payton, on track for an All-NBA career of his own, knew Jason could run an offense, but was he willing to play mad D? The lessons were doled out in elbows and measured in pain. "I used to beat up on him to make him tough," Payton laughs. "He used to go home and tell his mother. But he'd come back every day and do something different to stop me from what I was doing to him."

"I learned from the best," Jason likes to say.

The first recruiting letter arrived when the boy was 14, before he even got his feet wet as a freshman at St. Joseph of Notre Dame. "Already?" Jason thought. He knew he was good, but this was stupid. Fast forward a couple of seasons and the recruiters look pretty smart. With Jason at the helm, the Pilots are practically unbeatable. Two state championships—not bad for school with only 600 kids. Coach Frank LaPorte has to build in time for his point guard's pregame and post-game autograph sessions. Other kids are wearing Jason Kidd t-shirts. Outside of Joe Montana and the Bash Brothers, he's the biggest thing in the Bay Area.

By the start of his senior year, Jason narrowed his "official" list of college choices to five. Cal was not on the list. Jason never "officially" visited Cal. Jason had zero contact with Cal coach Lou

KIDD STUFF

FACT: Jason's favorite sport was soccer until the third grade...when the fourth graders asked him to join their basketball team.

FACT: As a teenager, Jason's patented move was to dish to a shooter, slice his way to the basket, then dunk the rebound.

FACT: Jason's younger sisters are Denise and Kim. His mother, Anne, worked for a bank; his father, Steve, was an airline supervisor.

FACT: The best thing to happen to Jason while playing in Phoenix was meeting his wife, Joumana, a local television reporter. They celebrated the birth of twins in the fall of 2001.

KIDD'S STUFF

By Annette John-Hall

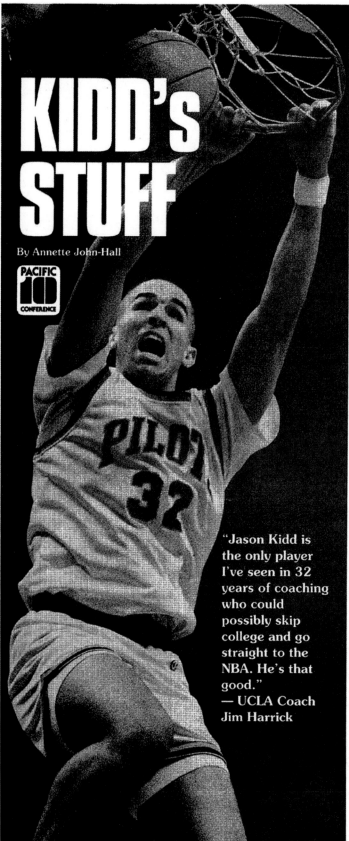

"Jason Kidd is the only player I've seen in 32 years of coaching who could possibly skip college and go straight to the NBA. He's that good."
— UCLA Coach Jim Harrick

The question regarding Pacific 10 basketball isn't whether the conference will have three teams in the top 10, as it did last year.

Or whether it breaks a three-year pattern and sends more than four teams to the NCAA tournament.

It's not even whether the Pac-10 can produce four first-round NBA draft picks, as it did last year.

Here's the question everybody asks regarding Pac-10 basketball this season: Is Jason Kidd enough to help Cal win its first conference title in 33 years?

Kidd, the Golden Bears' golden recruit, is a 6-foot, 4-inch package of passing, shooting and ballhandling theatrics out of St. Joseph of Alameda, a few miles down the road from Cal's Berkeley campus.

"Jason Kidd is the only player I've seen in 32 years of coaching who could possibly skip college and go straight to the NBA," UCLA Coach Jim Harrick said. "He's that good."

And that confident. "Cal will reach the NCAA Final Four within two years," Kidd said when announcing his choice of colleges.

Kidd, along with 6'2" guard Jerod Haase, the Nevada Player of the Year from South Lake Tahoe High, should help catapult Lou Campanelli's Cal squad from last season's ninth-place finish to the conference's upper division this year.

Not since the days of Phil Chenier in the early '70s has the Berkeley campus been so abuzz with anticipation over an incoming freshman. In Kidd's case, that anticipation is warranted.

"He's a 6'4" Magic," Harrick said.

That said, the Bears figure to improve on last year's 10-18 record. How much they impro[ve] on Kidd making a succe[ss] tion to the college gam[e] and it's a big if — seni[or] Brian Hendrick can su[c] come back from last se[ason] kneecap surgery.

The Bears will be he[avy] and experience. Four f[reshmen] Lamond Murray, Al Gr[ay] Roberts and Monty Bu[ckley] into starting roles last s[eason]

"Freshmen and soph[omores] be our team, but we di[d] experience and I hope [it pays] off," Campanelli said. "[When Hendrick] comes back, I like our [chances] that's something we do[n't have] yet."

Campanelli does kno[w] the future is even brigh[ter than] coming season's outlo[ok]

"I commend Jason f[or the] courage to walk away f[rom] the more established na[tional pro-] grams in order to be pa[rt of the]

building process at Cal," said Campanelli, entering his eighth season with the Bears. "I think he realized he can be a part of something special."

The Bears, though vastly improved, will still be a longshot for the Pac-10 crown this season. UCLA has the talent to repeat, but the Bruins should get a down-to-the-wire test from Arizona, which has won or shared the title five of the last seven seasons.

Mitch Butler, a 6'5" swingman who averaged eight points and 4.3 rebounds last season, figures, as the only returning starter for UCLA, to get just as much a chance as Kidd at Cal to mold his team.

"I think he can be the leader of the team but what he does on the floor will determine that," Harrick said.

Still, the Bruins have enough quality stepping in to be as explosive as last year's Elite Eight squad.

Lute Olson also is replacing quality with quality at Arizona and speed with greater speed on a team that will be revved by guards Khalid Reeves and Damon Stoudamire.

Kidd and Cal figure to be in the next grouping with USC (24-8 last year and No. 8 nationally but George Raveling's three-guard offense is no longer a surprise), Arizona State (super-quick, nine returning veterans) and Oregon State (underrated 6'-11" Scott Haskin heads four returning starters). Counting downward to 10, that leaves Oregon, Washington, Stanford and Washington State.

It's a grouping the University of California will vacate this year. The only question is how high is up.

"I want to put Cal on the map," Kidd says. "I hope to bring excite-[ment]

JASON KIDD

COLLEGE STATS

SEASON	G	MIN	FG%	FT%	RPG	APG	PPG
1992–93	29	922	46.3	65.7	4.9	7.7	13.0
1993–94	30	1,053	47.2	69.2	6.9	9.1	16.7

FRESHMAN OF THE YEAR 1993
NCAA STEALS LEADER 1993
ALL-AMERICAN 1994
NCAA ASSISTS LEADER 1994

Campanelli. So what did he do? Jason chose Cal. In the soul-crushing world of college basketball recruiting, it was the ultimate no-look pass.

Jason picked the Golden Bears because they were close to home—close enough, in fact, that he had been hanging around their gym and working out with their varsity players. He liked how the college guys turned his passes into buckets. Jason did not like how Campanelli abused his teammates, and stood up to him. Out went Campanelli, in came assistant Todd Bozeman, five years removed from a gig as a FedEx driver. Now that's power. A few weeks later, Jason carried Cal into the 1993 NCAA Tournament and hit a couple of amazing game-winners. The first came in a forest of seven-footers wearing LSU jerseys. The second derailed the Duke Blue

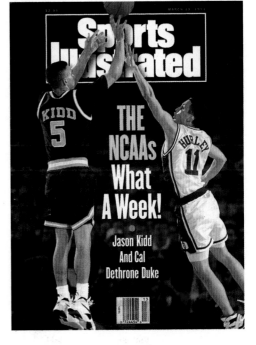

Devils on their way to a three-peat, and earned Jason the cover of SPORTS ILLUSTRATED.

After a sensational sophomore season that saw him lead the nation in assists, Jason decided to go pro.

LEFT: By the time Jason got to Cal he had already been the subject of several feature stories, like this one in COLLEGE SPORTS. He also had his own trading card while he was still a teenager. ABOVE: Jason makes the cover of SPORTS ILLUSTRATED with his big game against Duke.

2 TAKING THE POINT

Jason was selected by the Dallas Mavericks with the second pick in the 1994 NBA Draft, right behind Big Dog Robinson and in front of Grant Hill. Jason became the third J on a young and talented Dallas squad that included Jimmy Jackson and Jamal Mashburn. The team had mutinied under coach Quinn Buckner the year before, paving the way for a return by veteran coach Dick Motta. With a fresh start and Jason at the point, the Mavs were looking marvelous. Where once Dallas players had moped down the court, they now sprinted—knowing that the ball might come their way without notice. Jackson and Mashburn had 50-point games, the team was winning, and Jason was doing all those amazing things that never show up in the box score. Comeback vic-

> " I always feel the last five minutes is when the game is won or lost. "
>
> • **Jason Kidd**

In the years before he arrived in New Jersey, Jason's career had its ups and downs. One of the major highlights was leading Team USA to a gold medal at the 2000 Olympics in Sydney, Australia.

tories were his specialty; 25 percent of Big D's victories came after rallying from double-digit deficits, including a couple of times when the team trailed by more than 20.

Jason's presence improved the Mavs by 23 games—no first-year guard had ever made a bigger impact. Had Jackson not been felled by a season-ending ankle injury 51 games in, who knows what the final numbers would have been? For Jason's part, he shared Rookie of the Year honors with Grant Hill and won raves for his defensive work.

> "Jason is one of the most advanced and talented players to come into the league in a long time."
>
> • **Charles Barkley**

Alas, the days of wine and roses did not last in Dallas. The fourth J—jealousy—reared its ugly head as Jimmy and Jamal began feuding, then Jason and Jimmy began grappling over control of the ball. Bad ideas, all. Without a veteran leader to step up and say what needed to be said, Jason attempted to fill the void but said all the wrong things. Disharmony dragged Dallas down, and the Mavs descended into Clipper territory with a record of 26–56. Jason didn't realize it at the time, but this was an important part of his NBA education. You can't fully understand what it takes to win until you see all the things that lead a talented team to lose.

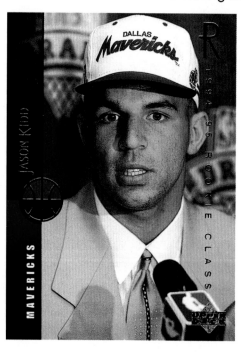

Fast forward again, this time to Phoenix. It's the day after Christmas, 1996, and Jason is a human stocking-stuffer for fans of the Suns. The trade sends Sam Cassell, A.C. Green and Michael Finley to the Mavs—by Dallas standards a darn good deal. Jason is installed as the franchise player, the departure of Green gives Phoenix tons of room under the salary cap, and the future looks bright. But Jason is steamed. The Mavs, disappointed he could not

ABOVE: Jason's Upper Deck rookie card, which shows him on draft day, became an instant hit with collectors. **RIGHT:** As this *SPORTS ILLUSTRATED FOR KIDS* cover shows, the 1996 trade to the Suns was big news among his young fans.

raise the team's play by force of will, are questioning that will. Now that he's gone, they are quietly trashing him to anyone willing to listen.

By this point in his young career, Jason had learned a valuable lesson: If you're not there to defend yourself, let your play do your talking. In his first game in a Phoenix uniform he dished out nine assists and hauled down seven rebounds in 20 minutes before a fractured collarbone sent him to the sidelines. Jason came back to play in 32 more games in 1996–97, then logged 82 in 1997–98—during

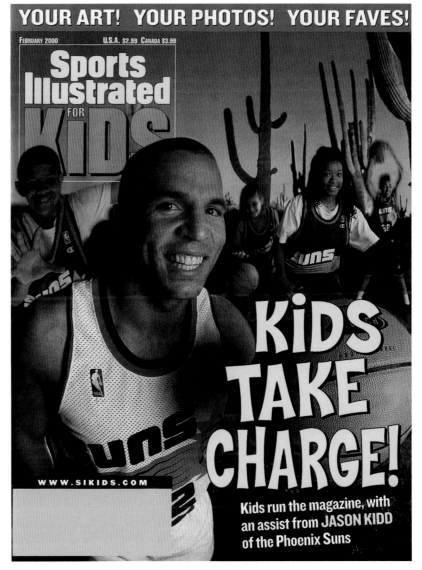

which Phoenix finished with a sparkling 56–26 record. Eight of Jason's teammates averaged nine or more points a game.

Jason continued to grow as a player with the Suns, leading the NBA in assists two years in a row and making First-team All-NBA. Yet despite the presence of All-Star caliber teammates like Penny Hardaway, Antonio McDyess, Clifford Robinson and Tom Gugliotta, Jason could not get the Suns past the second round in the playoffs. Every year it was something else. In 1997, they were beaten by a strong Seattle squad. In 1998, they fell to Tim Duncan and San Antonio in the first round. In 1999, after a lockout-shortened season, they were swept by Portland. In 2000, the Suns dumped the defending champion Spurs in the first round, only to lose to the Lakers.

Something had to give.

During the first half of the 2000–01 season, the Phoenix papers carried dramatic headlines accusing Hardaway of waving a gun in a woman's face, top scorer Robinson picked up a DUI, and Jason was charged with smacking his wife, Joumana, during a January 18 domestic dispute. The couple patched up their differences and assured fans they planned to stay together (they had twins the following fall) and Jason made an emotional public apology. But in the eyes of Phoenix management, the damage was done. When the Suns spit the bit in the playoffs again (this time to Sacramento), the phone calls began.

The knock on Jason was that he wasn't "up" enough. Owner Jerry Colangelo felt his understated style did not bring the fans out of their seats. This irritated Jason, whose nature is to attack, attack, attack until an opponent proves it can stop him. The problem in Phoenix was a lack of finishers. It's one thing to fast break at every opportunity, but when your teammates can't or won't take the ball to the hole, it's silly to force the issue. The Suns probably knew this, but dealing Jason was the best way to dump the excess baggage he had accumulated in his years in Arizona. The trade, made a few days after the June draft, was a swap with the Nets for Stephon Marbury, the running, gunning, fist-pumping player Jason could never—no, *would* never—be.

> "Jason gets you the ball when you need to score."
>
> • **Jamal Mashburn**

ABOVE: Jason turns the corner and looks for an open man. He changed his hair color on a dare from his wife, Joumana. **RIGHT:** A card collector as a kid, Jason had a blast posing for this cover with Jamal Mashburn and Jim Jackson.

3 FOOT OF THE MOUNTAIN

For 25 years there have been two absolute truths in the NBA: there's no such thing as traveling on a layup and no one wants to play in New Jersey. Actually, Jason's anger at being traded to the Nets had more to do with how he learned about it than where he was headed. Instead of getting a call from the team, he heard it like the rest of Phoenix, through the media. However, at

> ## Jason, by far, to me, is the best point guard in the NBA.
>
> ### • Penny Hardaway

his press conference the next day, Jason displayed maturity that had sometimes eluded him during tough times. With Joumana by his side, he answered questions evenly and directly. Did his January arrest play a role in the trade? "That could be," Jason responded, "But most likely people will say it's a basketball decision."

Across the continent, Nets president Rod Thorn focused on what his new guard brought to the party. "Our three biggest problems last year were rebounding, defense, and team chemistry," he said. "With one trade, we got significantly better in all those areas."

Jason uses his left hand to score on Jalen Rose of the Indiana Pacers. By the time the Nets and Pacers met in the postseason, Rose had been traded.

Jason had to turn things over in his mind a little before realizing that he might be looking at a fresh start. The Secaucus swamps notwithstanding, New Jersey hardly seemed the quagmire people made it out to be. On the contrary, New Jersey's lackluster record in 2000–01 was not due to a paucity of talent. Kerry Kittles and Kenyon Martin were superb finishers—when they were healthy, of course. Kittles was coming back from reconstructive surgery to his right knee, Martin from a broken right fibula. Keith Van Horn needed to remember he was a 6–10 forward, not a 5–10 shooting guard. Off the bench, the team's role players weren't bad either, especially guard Lucious Harris and forward Aaron Williams. Both were veterans who had spent more years than they cared to remember on bad teams. They would do just about anything for a chance to contribute to a winner.

According to Thorn and his coach, Byron Scott, good health and solid leadership were the only ingredients missing from the Nets. That's where Jason came in. Forgetting the odd broken bone, he was an ironman who wanted to take the court every night. And unlike his predecessor, Marbury, he actually appeared to like his teammates. There were few players in the league as upbeat and positive as Jason. Indeed, he went so far as to predict he'd take this team to the playoffs.

> "Kidd's strength as a defender is in his anticipation."
>
> • **Reggie Theus**

ABOVE: The Nets' fine play in the early going landed them on the cover of *SLAM* magazine. RIGHT: Kerry Kittles launches a jumper. His return to health was a major part of the Nets' success in 2001–02.

"Most people think I'm crazy," he said at the time. "But sometimes you got to be crazy to be successful. I'm not trying to be politically correct. I really think it's great for me, and also great for the Nets. I think the opportunity is a challenge, and that challenge is to win ball-games. I'm ready."

Those words were music to Scott's ears. Despite what he and Jason thought, the New Jersey roster did not exactly have opponents quaking in their boots. Kittles, Van Horn and Martin were still trying to find their way in the NBA, and big man Todd MacCulloch was, well, big. A quartet of rookies—Richard Jefferson, Jason Collins, Brandon Armstrong, and Brian Scalabrine—would vie for playing time. Williams and Harris were the main men off the bench. On the surface, this was the same team that finished 26–56 the year before. How much difference could a new point guard make?

> "We got a person in here who wasn't gonna turn his head when you missed a shot."
>
> • **Lucious Harris**

Scott had his own ideas on this issue. The night before training camp opened the coach asked Jason to say a few words. You're not losers, Jason told his teammates. Work hard, and we can win as a team. Everyone in the room was on the edge of his seat. "I think a bunch of guys were ready to go out and play right then, they were so happy," recalls Van Horn. "That night had a big impact on every-thing else that happened."

Slowly but surely, Scott molded the Nets into Jason's image. Dig in on defense, hit the boards on both ends, and push the ball down the court to keep your enemies huffing and puffing. This was Jason's game, and with Jason running the show it was a fun game for every-one else to play.

With the mood in camp upbeat and the team prognosis steadily improving, Jason began sidling over to New Jersey's three stars and finding out what made them tick. He found Kittles and Van Horn played better when he built up their confidence. He saw how Martin delighted in learning the little tricks that squeezed the most out of his talent. Jason also let the rookies know what their contributions would have to be if the team was going to make the playoffs. And he

Jason looked forward to playing in the East, where guards and forwards reign. The opportunity to play against an un-retired Michael Jordan was an added bonus.

NET RESULTS

Jason Kidd is the latest in a long line of prolific Net point guards. Here's the dish on their best assist seasons:

PLAYER	ASSISTS	YEAR
Jason Kidd	595	2001–02
Stephon Marbury	622	1999–00
Sam Cassell	603	1997–98
Chris Childs	548	1995–96
Kenny Anderson	784	1993–94
Mookie Blaylock	492	1991–92
Lester Conner	604	1988–89
Michael Richardson	669	1984–85
Eddie Jordan	557	1979–80
Kevin Porter	801	1977–78
Bill Melchionni	672	1970–71

assured bench warmers Harris and Williams that they would be logging important minutes all season long.

The Nets may not have looked like a 50-win team when they broke camp, but they were starting to feel like one.

Their biggest challenge was to convince their fans to come watch them play. Less than 9,000 showed up for the season opener against the Indiana Pacers. They gave Jason a warm welcome, along with the rest of the players. Minutes later, as the Nets began falling behind, you could feel the chill run through the Continental Airlines Arena. Man, here we go again.

As the final 12 minutes began counting down, something amazing happened. In past seasons each second was little more than a death knell for the Nets when they trailed in the fourth quarter. But this time they began chipping away at the Pacers' 11-point lead. Jason would not let his teammates quit. He led a furious comeback and the Nets won 103–97. The gleam of sheer joy on the faces of the players was amplified by their own disbelief. Wins like this were few and far between in seasons past.

Six of New Jersey's next eight opponents fell to Kidd & Company. Included in that stretch, which catapulted the club to the top of the division standings, was a tough win against the Celtics in Boston, and a 26-point blowout of the haughty Knicks. Jason piled up 15 assists in that game, spreading the ball around to all of his teammates so they could get in on the fun. The Nets also beat up on Seattle 106–94. Jason got the better of his buddy Payton with 16 points and 13 assists.

"Jason is a great passer who looks to get others involved."

• **Keith Van Horn**

Kenyon Martin throws one down. His improved play in the middle was a key to New Jersey's early-season success.

Scott was asked afterwards to compare the two point guards. "The only difference," he smiled, "is Gary talks a lot."

Jason preferred to do his talking off the court. He was genuinely excited by what he was seeing from his teammates. "I think this team down the road will be the best team I've played on," he said. "Athletic-wise and talent-wise, it will be by far the best team. And if we can keep everybody healthy, it will be the most fun team."

Jason was a genius. When guys like Van Horn and Kittles heard him speak about them in such glowing terms to the media, they worked a little harder in practice and walked a little taller during games.

Of course, Jason had been on rolls before. And he knew how quickly things could fall apart. He cautioned his jubilant teammates that they hadn't been tested yet. That would occur on their November swing through the NBA's western cities. Sure enough, the first game, in Denver, was a deflating loss. Jason shot 1 of 10 from beyond the arc, and shouldered most of the blame. The Nets fought back, literally, against the Jazz in Utah, as Scott got in Karl Malone's face when the Mailman objected to Martin's bullying of reserve John Crotty.

> "Jason Kidd is the second coming of Magic Johnson, only a shorter version. He's a guy who can carry you on his back. He uplifts his teammates just like Magic."
>
> • **Byron Scott**

After their win at the Delta Center, the Nets split their next two, against the Clippers and Kings. Jason recorded a pair of triple-doubles in those contests. When they got back home, the Nets were still perched atop the Atlantic Division.

Jason knew the next challenge would be a personal one. The Suns were due for a December visit, and he got it into his head that the best way to repay their unkindness would be to lead New Jersey to victory without scoring a single point. On paper it was a fine idea, but in reality he knew there would be shots he'd have to take. Still, Jason racked up 11 assists before making his first bucket. With Joumana and his three-year-old son, T.J., in the stands, he dominated all night in a 106–97 victory.

Jason defends against Stephon Marbury. His superb game sent a message to the Suns.

As the Nets stretched their division lead, fans began finding their way back to Exit 16W—a handful a night at first, but slowly, steadily, they came. They cheered for a team that made the sharp cut, anticipated the stray rebound, and threw the extra pass. They oooh'd and aaah'd at twisting drives and pull-up jumpers. They saw players helping on defense in ways that only show up in one stat: wins. A little of Jason was definitely beginning to rub off.

Scott could barely contain himself sometimes as he witnessed his team's metamorphosis. Kittles was regaining his stroke and shooting with confidence. Van Horn was mixing it up inside as he had in college, then sneaking outside for wide-open three-pointers. The role players were actually playing roles, and playing them well, no less. And Kenyon Martin? Well, he was just one bad dude. He roamed the lane on defense like he owned it. Trespass on his turf, and be prepared to pay the price.

What they all had in common was a focus on the good things they could accomplish together. They weren't sure how it would all turn out, but they sure enjoyed rewriting the story. "There's a lot of heart on this ballclub," confirms Kidd. "There are guys who have been through a heck of a lot in this locker room. The good thing is no one talks about the past. Everyone is looking to the future."

The team's next big game came in mid-December, against the Minnesota Timberwolves. It was being billed as a battle between the league's two up-and-coming teams, although anyone who knew their history wasn't buying it just yet. Both clubs had immense talent, yet had produced mostly disappointment in the recent past. Still, it was a heck of a game, and 12,000-plus turned out. Jason stunned the T-Wolves when he came out gunning, and the Nets built a 19-point lead early in the fourth quarter. Then Kevin Garnett and Company caught fire and tied the score in the final seconds, forcing overtime. Here was a game the Nets used to lose four out of five times. Jason would hear none of that. He and Martin combined for a half-dozen points a piece in the extra period and closed out Minnesota 117–112.

Though hardly a stoic, Scott was unusually ebullient when the post-game questions came around to the subject of Jason Kidd. "If he's not the best in the league, then you all are crazy," Scott told the assembled throng. "He wants the ball when the game's one the line."

Jason and his son T.J. hang out at a Nets practice.

4 THIRST FOR *FIRST*

The Nets were starting to scare people. When you missed a shot against this team, you had to turn and run. If you didn't, someone was going to beat you down the court, and Jason was going to find him. And despite all the dismissive winks and knowing glances around the league, the team was showing no sign of loosening its stranglehold on first place. Among basketball people, there was grudging acknowledgement that Jason had finally found a new level for his game, and that—if the season ended tomorrow—there was no player more deserving of the MVP.

With the All-Star break approaching, the Nets got their biggest crowd (20,049) of the season when Michael Jordan and the Wizards came to town. Years earlier, Jordan had invited Jason to play a round of golf with him. Jason was amazed how competitive Michael was—in everything.

> "No one anticipates like he does. When he grabs a rebound, he's taking a picture of the court before he hits the ground."
>
> • **Kerry Kittles**

Jason blows his trademark kiss at the basket before attempting a free throw.

Richard Jefferson dunks against the Celtics. His emergence as an effective role player was one of the year's big stories.

What he thought would be a pleasant day on the links turned out to be a nerve-wracking lesson in pressure golf. Jason was hardly surprised when Jordan announced his return to the NBA. Frankly, he didn't understand how the superstar could stay away. Well, now it was Jason's turn to repay an old golf debt. He tore through the Washington defense and gave the fans a night to remember, as the Nets routed Washington by 44 points.

"Going crazy after every play, that's not me."

• **Jason Kidd**

Despite stellar numbers (14.3 points, 9.9 assists, 7.1 rebounds, 2.15 steals and a 35–12 record) Jason was not voted into the starting lineup for the East All-Stars. When an injury forced Vince Carter off the floor for the opening tip, Jason was picked to replace him. Meanwhile, everyone at the All-Star Weekend love fest had one question for Jason: Could the Nets get it done down the stretch? "Our mindset is to play the way we have been all season and things will take of themselves," he answered. "We will just go out there, have fun, and do our best."

More than a quarter-century had passed since the once-proud ABA Nets joined the NBA. During that time, the team had failed to win even a single division title. In their best year, the Nets finished with 49 wins. There were no history majors on the 2002 club, but to a man everyone was aware that they were approaching uncharted territory. Perhaps that explains the mini-collapse the team suffered after the break. Jason was as guilty as anyone, shooting a miserable 7-of-34 in losses to the Hawks and Pistons.

By this time, however, the Nets had too many wins under their belts to start seriously doubting themselves. They righted the ship and reeled off six straight wins. Not even a second late-season slump could erode their confidence. Jason recorded his seventh triple-double of the season in a 97–78 victory over Miami. It was the team's 41st win, which guaranteed them a .500 season. With 17 games left, they still had a shot at 50.

The last time the Nets won their division, Dr. J was hawking Dr. Pepper!

"There's nothing better than making a pass that gives someone an easy hoop."

• **Jason Kidd**

NBA STATS

SEASON	TEAM	G	MIN	FG%	FT%	RPG	APG	PPG
1994–95	Mavs	79	2,668	38.5	69.8	5.4	7.7	11.7
1995–96	Mavs	81	3,034	38.1	69.2	6.8	9.7	16.6
1996–97	Mavs/Suns	55	1,964	40.3	67.9	4.5	9.0	10.9
1997–98	Suns	82	3,118	41.6	79.9	6.2	9.1	11.6
1998–99	Suns	50	2,060	44.4	75.7	6.8	10.8	16.9
1999–00	Suns	67	2,616	40.9	82.9	7.2	10.1	14.3
2000–01	Suns	77	3,065	41.1	81.4	6.4	9.8	16.9
2001–02	Nets	82	3,056	39.1	81.4	7.3	9.9	14.7

#2 DRAFT CHOICE *1994*
CO-ROOKIE OF THE YEAR *1995*
NBA ASSISTS LEADER *1999*

3-TIME ALL-NBA
5-TIME NBA ALL-STAR

Jason and the Nets shifted into overdrive. They took eight of their next 11, setting up a key home contest against Washington. A win would give them 50 for the season and clinch the Atlantic Division title. The Nets beat the Wizards by 13, with Jason scoring 21 points and dishing out a dozen assists. Chants of "MVP" cascaded down from every part of the arena, as the fans reveled in their team's history-making moment. "He was his normal incredible self," said Rod Thorn after the game.

The team won twice more for a final record of 52–30. Jason's numbers—14.2 ppg, 9.9 apg, and 7.3 rpg—were excellent, but barely hinted at his impact. The league had once watched in awe as he improved the Mavericks by 23 games in his rookie year, but this was something entirely different. This bordered on the fantastic. When Jason and his teammates began talking about making it to the NBA Finals, you almost wanted to believe them.

Jason talks things over with coach Byron Scott. Scott depended on him to be a coach on the floor, and Jason rarely disappointed.

5 SECOND SEASON

As the league geared up for the playoffs, Jason's fans were getting ready for the MVP announcement. With his stunning performance, Jason had eclipsed the early-season favorite, Shaquille O'Neal. So had Tim Duncan of the Spurs. Clearly, the voting would be close between these two. Jason's mind was on other things. Though he'd never admit it, every year when the post-season starts, he replays all those first-round losses.

The first round this year would bring the Indiana Pacers, a club with a mix of youth and experience, as well as a dangerous X factor: Reggie Miller. Miller will probably make the Hall of Fame off of the playoff games he had against New Jersey's cross-Hudson rivals. Byron Scott, a former teammate, did not want Reggie adding to his post-season résumé against the Nets.

There were other worries. In Jermaine O'Neal and Jamal Tinsley, Indiana had a couple of youngsters who could do real damage. And

> "When we win, it's going to be as a team. It's not going to be something Jason has done singlehandedly."
>
> • **Jason Kidd**

Jason rises over Jeff Foster of the Pacers in first-round playoff action.
Jason made the basket and drew the foul.

then there was the issue of New Jersey's halfcourt offense, which had failed to distinguish itself during the regular season. Come playoff time, you need to bump and grind if you want to win, and most scouts questioned whether the surprising Nets had the mettle to do this. The team's free throw shooting was nothing to brag about, either. Although the Nets were favored to take the Pacers in their best-of-five series, many wondered whether they could. And few believed they'd make it out of the second round.

After New Jersey dropped the opener at home, 89–83, you could practically hear people jumping off the bandwagon. Every doom-and-gloom prediction had come true, the Nets had lost their home-court advantage, and Jason was to blame. In tense moments he seemed to be looking for his shot instead of his teammates. Stephon Marbury déjà vu. What Jason was doing, however, turned out to be a pretty smart move. Sensing the guys were a little jittery, he took the big shots himself so they could concentrate on the easier parts of the game. Although the Nets lost Game 1, they played a smooth and relaxed Game 2, and coasted to a 16-point win to knot the series.

Indiana coach Isiah Thomas, once a pretty fair point guard himself, saw what Jason was doing and realized he had his hands full. Not only had he loosened up his fellow Nets, but he had new gained confidence in his own scoring ability. Thomas and his players claimed they would rather have Jason shoot than pass, but they were unconvincing. After he scored 25 in an 85–84 win in Game 3, it was clear the havoc he was creating among the Pacer defenders was taking its toll.

> "I'm not a shoot first, ask questions later point guard."
>
> • **Jason Kidd**

After the Pacers staved off elimination in Game 4, the series returned to the Meadowlands, where Jason and Reggie Miller took turns topping one another in a thrilling "refuse to lose" contest. The Nets raced to an early lead, but Indiana closed the gap at the half. The game seesawed into the fourth quarter, until Jason sparked New Jersey to a 10-point bulge. The Pacers fought back, however, and now it was Miller Time.

With just a few seconds remaining and the Nets ahead by three, Indiana grabbed a rebound off a missed free throw by Richard Jefferson and hurried the ball to Miller. He launched an off-balance 30-footer that banked into the basket at the buzzer to force overtime.

Ah, but now it was Jason's turn. He singlehandedly kept New Jersey in the game, answering each Indiana basket with a clutch shot of his own. The game went into a second extra period. The fans watched breathlessly as Jason kept coming at the Pacers. Two jumpers gave the Nets a five-point lead, and they finally were able to pull away, 120–109.

Up next was Charlotte. An athletic team with a versatile front line, the Hornets presented problems for the Nets. But New Jersey caught a break when an illness sidelined Jamal Mashburn. His absence placed more of the scoring burden on point guard Baron Davis, who would already have his work cut out for him dealing with Jason. The Nets took the first two games at Continental Airlines Arena in impressive fashion. Everyone was contributing.

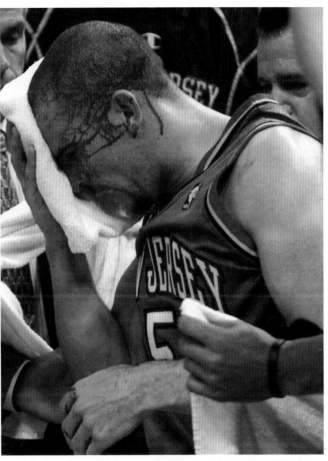

Jason is a mess after colliding with David Wesley in the Charlotte series. He came back to key a Game 4 victory.

Lucious Harris came off the bench to lead the team in scoring in Game 2, and Van Horn was a rebounding fool. The only thing Nets fans could complain about was the news that Tim Duncan had edged Jason for the MVP award.

"I think it's ridiculous," said Byron Scott. "What Jason has done for our team and where we have come from, I don't understand it."

The MVP debate was still raging when the Nets took the floor for Game 3 in Charlotte. Just before halftime, Jason clunked head with David Wesley going after a loose ball. The blow opened a gash over Jason's right eye that required 15 stitches to close. He returned midway through the third quarter looking like a beaten prize fighter. The Nets lost 115–97, and braced for the possibility that Jason might be woozy for the next game.

Perish the thought. Jason not only played in Game 4, he carried New Jersey with 13 fourth-quarter points to key an 89–79 victory.

The Nets closed out the series three nights later with their fearless point guard leading the way again.

The Nets now stood four wins away from the NBA Finals. In their path stood the Boston Celtics, a team with two huge stars in Paul Pierce and Antoine Walker, a veteran point man in ex-Net Kenny Anderson, and a good defensive center in Tony Battie. On paper, the Nets' superior depth gave them an edge in the series, but that would only come into play if they could contain Boston two scorers. Prior to the series, the Nets still felt like a team searching for respect. Byron Scott hammered home this point, and told his players that the only way to change people's minds was to keep on winning. Much would depend on Kenyon Martin in this series. He had to control the boards.

The Nets won Game 1 at home, 104–97. Jason did it all in the victory, posting his first triple-double of the playoffs with 18 points, 13 rebounds, and 11 assists. The Celtics bounced back in Game 2 with a 93–86 win, despite another triple-double by Kidd. The good news for New Jersey was that Martin was doing a superb job on Pierce.

Kidd and his mates arrived in Boston determined to regain the homecourt advantage. They were on track in Game 3, when they opened a seemingly insurmountable lead in the second half, going up by as many as 26 points. No team in playoff history had ever overcome such a large deficit. But the Celtics finally started to click,

ABOVE: Paul Pierce celebrates Boston's amazing fourth-quarter comeback in Game 3.
RIGHT: Jason lets the Fleet Center crowd know who's in charge after New Jersey's Game 4 victory.

PERSONAL BESTS

Here's a look at Jason's best statistical performances as a pro:

POINTS 43
3-POINTERS 8
ASSISTS 25
STEALS 6
REBOUNDS 16
BLOCKS 4

Pierce went wild, and the Nets went ice cold. Incredibly, the Celtics went ahead with less than a minute remaining, and nailed down a 94–90 win. Jason, held scoreless in the final 12 minutes, wore the goat horns. His teammates had looked to him at crunch time and he had let them down. Jason accepted blame without complaint.

What *did* bother him was the shabby treatment his wife and son received from the fans at the Fleet Center. Throughout the game, Joumana and T.J. were taunted by the people sitting near them at courtside. Jason actually feared for their safety. It proved another motivating factor for New Jersey as the series wore on.

Game 4 was a good one. The Nets grabbed an early lead, but the Celtics cut their advantage to six at the half. Jason helped extend that lead by nine points in the third quarter, but again Boston came back. Jason took over in the final period and urged his fellow Nets to step up their D. On offense, they canned one tough shot after another. When the buzzer sounded on New Jersey's 94–92 win, Jason stomped around the Fleet Center, telling the Boston fans exactly what he thought of them. "I was tired of being humble," he says. "As a veteran of a team, sometimes you have to speak out."

With the series tied at 2–2, the Nets felt revitalized. They smoked the Celts in the final quarter of Game 5, then put the series on ice in Boston with a 96–88 victory. For the first time in franchise history, New Jersey was headed to the NBA Finals. With 15 points, 13 rebounds, and 13 assists, Kidd became the first player in 35 years to record three triple-doubles in a playoff series.

Jason and Kenyon Martin embrace after the final buzzer sounds on their Game 6 win over the Celtics. For the first time since joining the NBA, the Nets were in the finals. The victory was front page news in the New York papers.

4 STAR ★ ★ ★ ★ FINAL

DAILY ● NEWS

www.nydailynews.com NEW YORK'S HOMETOWN NEWSPAPER Saturday, June 1, 200

Jason Kidd celebrates victory over Celtics last night in Boston. SEE SPORTS

NOTHIN' BUT NETS!

6 FINALLY!

Be careful what you wish for. It's true in life, and it's true in the NBA. The Nets were on their way to the finals, but they didn't know yet whom they would face. Los Angeles and Sacramento were going to Game 7 in the Western Conference final and Jason and his teammates watched with mixed emotions. They had battled both teams to two-game splits during the regular season. Both teams, they knew, would be prohibitive favorites.

The fighter in Jason told him he wanted to dethrone the defending champs. When the Lakers eked out an overtime victory against the Kings, the Nets had the opportunity to do just that. Now the really hard work began.

"Dynasty" was the word on the tip of tongue of fans around Los Angeles—and they weren't talking about trashy '80s television. The Nets were the proverbial bump in the road on the way to a third-straight Laker championship. So sure were basketball people that

> "It's been one of those destiny-type things that has taken place this season."
> • **Jason Kidd**

Jason catches his breath in Game 1 of the NBA Finals, as Lakers star Kobe Bryant looks on.

ABOVE: Kobe and Jason battled hard in the finals. Here Kobe lands in the lap of a photographer. RIGHT: Jason searches for a way to solve the Lakers.

New Jersey would not survive. Indeed, newspaper headlines called the Nets the "Ultimate Underdog."

They did have a point. The Lakers possess the fiercest one-two punch in the NBA. Kobe Bryant is approaching Jordan status, what with his high-flying dunks and go-for-the-jugular instincts. Shaquille O'Neal is just plain unmanageable. Keeping these two on track is Phil Jackson, he of the ponderous Zen musings and Holzman basketball fundamentals.

L.A.'s 2001–02 supporting cast left something to be desired, however. Beyond Robert Horry, Rick Fox and Derek Fisher was a bench full of question marks. If Byron Scott could force Phil to play these guys, the Nets would have more than a fighting chance. Jason would be the key. He would have to throw New Jersey's high-speed transition game into another gear and wear down the big, bad Lakers.

In the days leading up to Game 1, Jason had one thing in mind: Bring it on. "This is dynasty versus destiny," he said with a grin.

Against a team with Shaq and Kobe, there's only so much one man can do. Yet Jason had done so much to this point that nothing seemed impossible. Alas, Net fans had to do a reality check when the Lakers ran up a 23-point advantage in the early going. For the first time in a long time, you saw panic in the eyes of the New Jersey players.

But there was Jason, controlling the game again and chipping away at the lead. Little by little, they cut Goliath down to size. Jason scored seven points in a 17–6 run that cut the deficit to 12 at the half. And in the final three periods, the Nets actually outscored the L.A. by a wide margin. For his part, Jason finished with a triple-double—his second in a row. Twice in the final minutes he brought the Nets within four, but L.A. survived the onslaught, as great teams do, and closed out the game.

> "He showed great leadership, all through the season and especially the postseason. He's led us all the way."
>
> • **Kerry Kittles**

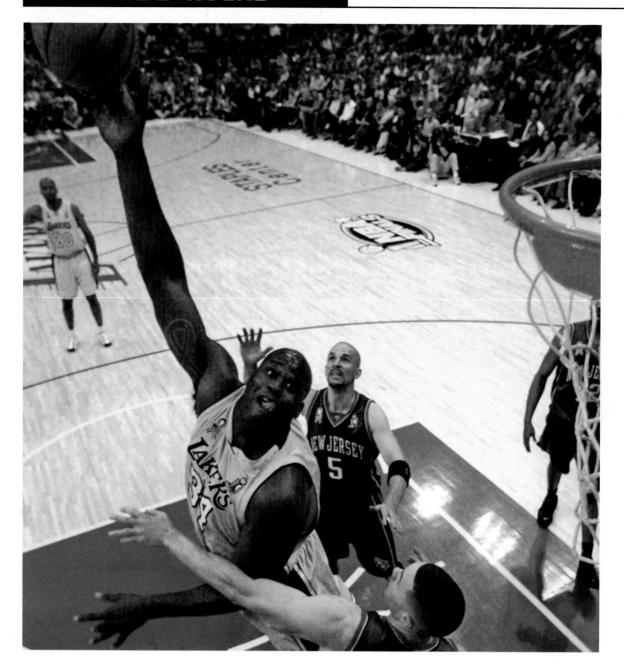

There was no celebrating. The Lakers filed solemnly under the stands. There in the faces of Phil Jackson and his players was that look so many other teams had taken back to the locker room during the year. The Nets were the real deal. The Lakers suddenly realized they'd be in for a fight.

How could they reasonably expect anything else? Jason Kidd makes it his business to thrive under these conditions. And as Jason goes, so go the Nets.

ABOVE: Jason watches as Shaq swoops to the hoop during the NBA Finals. Finding an answer to the big man was a major problem for the Nets.
RIGHT: Jason drives past Robert Horry in the series opener.

We have started to climb the mountain but we are not done. We can't put our foot down, we got to keep climbing, we've got a ways to go until we reach the top.

• Jason Kidd